NATURE'S TIMES

Edited by

Stephen Chambers

First published in Great Britain in 2003 by
POETRY NOW
Remus House,
Coltsfoot Drive,
Peterborough, PE2 9JX
Telephone (01733) 898101
Fax (01733) 313524

All Rights Reserved

Copyright Contributors 2003

HB ISBN 1 84460 928 6
SB ISBN 1 84460 929 4

FOREWORD

Although we are a nation of poets we are accused of not reading poetry, or buying poetry books. After many years of listening to the incessant gripes of poetry publishers, I can only assume that the books they publish, in general, are books that most people do not want to read.

Poetry should not be obscure, introverted, and as cryptic as a crossword puzzle: it is the poet's duty to reach out and embrace the world.

The world owes the poet nothing and we should not be expected to dig and delve into a rambling discourse searching for some inner meaning.

The reason we write poetry (and almost all of us do) is because we want to communicate: an ideal; an idea; or a specific feeling. Poetry is as essential in communication, as a letter; a radio; a telephone, and the main criterion for selecting the poems in this anthology is very simple: they communicate.

CONTENTS

This Time Of Day	Richard Gould	1
Intruder	Midge Bainbridge	2
The Birch Forest	Stephen Isaac	3
Mother Nature	Maxene Huntley	4
Where Do All The Seagulls Sleep?	Betty Gilman	5
On The Bank Of The Wye	Jean McPherson	6
Dinner Time Thoughts	R Law	7
The Magic Of The Purbeck Hills	Michael Davis	8
Locusts	Martin Winbolt-Lewis	9
Precious Times	Anne Edgar-Walters	10
Every Wave	Hugh Campbell	11
September	H Strangwige	12
Yahweh's Wonderful Creation	Miriam Elizabeth Black	13
Life Springs Eternal	May Strike	14
Nature's Customer	Zaynab Armstrong-Jones	15
Little Pidge Finds His Voice	Hilary Jean Clark	16
Roses In June	Nicky Young	18
November Metamorphosis	Margaret Hibbert	19
One January Afternoon	Glan Grey-Jones	20
Weatherwise	Hazel Sheppard	21
Global Warming	Olive May McIntosh-Stedman	22
To A Hedgehog	Joan Thompson	23
The Song In Us	S V Batten	24
Little Wren	David R Lucas	25
Halcyon Days	A Odger	26
Journeying Through Time	Lorna Tippett	27
A Rusting Gate With Hidden Depths	Doris Hoole	28
So Who?	D J Sim	29
Winter's War - Lost	Mike Pannell	30
Home	Martin D W Clarke	31
Summer Nights	Helene Birch	32
Gust	G F Snook	33
Silent Hour	Margaret Gurney	34
The Latest Arrival	Chris Creedon	35

Title	Author	Page
When The Wind Blows	M Fitzpatrick-Jones	36
The Moon	John W Garland	37
Plant Wisdom	Philippa Adburgham	38
Woodland Magic	Sharon Barnes	39
Allotments	Joy Bartelt	40
The Orchid	K M Baillie	41
Storm	R Murray	42
Skylark Days	John Whittock	44
Reflexes Of Awaken Nature	Ernest N Onuoha	45
Flowers	D Ramsey	46
Upon The Place Beneath	Hilary Moore	48
Autumn On Dogwood	Alan Murdoch	50
The Moors	J Rowley	51
The Balcony	Mariama Amoah	52
Mother Nature	J C Griffin	53
Rain	Annette Murphy	54
Weather	Grant Bayliss	55
Jack Frost Farewell	C H Baker	56
How I See You	L Fryer	57
Falling In The Scene	Samina Amjad	58
A Single Drop Of Rain	C A Keohane-Johnson	59
Almighty Sea	V Day	60
The River	Jeff Parks	61
Beloved Daisy	Elsie Scrowther	62
The Lonely Hillside	Lisa Christie	63
Mr Bumblebee	Marie Edwards	64
Shore Song	Andrew Hirst	65
Nature	Doreen Wilkinson	66
Look To The Countryside	C Hush	67
Pelican	Emma Cantillion	68
Our Surrounding World	Andrea M C Coleman	69
VI	Daniel Davies	70
Cocoon	Tia Thomson	71
Peregrinating Moon	Ron Hails	72
When The Wind Blows	Paula Natalie Turner	74
Tornado	Joy Morton	75
Illusion	Vera Morrill	76
A New Year, A New Beginning	Norma Pusey	77

Winter Rain	Pam Bridgwater	78
You August	Rosina M Drury	79
Facing The Fall	Di Bagshawe	80
Summer	Ian Fisher	81
New Year Noel	Malcolm Williams	82
Spring Will Come	Paul Gardner	83
September Song	Barbara Manning	84
Another New Year	L White	86
Winter Chill	S Joyce	87
Underneath The Apple Tree	Cameron McAulay	88
Winter Feelings	Phillipa Grundy	90
Naked Winter	K I Squires	91
Winter Night	Sylvia Fairclough	92
Winter	Diana Frewin	93
Spring	Rosemary Tester	94
Joys Of Spring	Jennifer Williams	95
Winter Bound	Jane England	96
Somerset	Tom Clarke	97
Rainy Autumn Evening	Ivy Allpress	98
Quickening New Life	Pamela Hopes	99
The Thunderstorm	Molly-Ann Kean	100
The Little Cherry Tree	Mary Waegner	101
Oxford, Winter 1962	Jeremy York	102
Pitiful Defiance	Jo Leak	103
Strained Relations	Alan Chesterfield	104
Snow	Joan M Jones	105
Winter	Phillip T Watson	106
The Autumn Leaves	John Michael Doherty	107
The Woods In Winter	Rosina Winiarski	108
Winter's Shroud	Pat Heppel	110
When The Wind Blows	N Daly	111
Autumn	Mary Hughes	112

THIS TIME OF DAY

At this time of day,
And in such a certain light,
The trees can take on
Shapes and shadows
Never envisaged or intended
By their creator.

The silvery dusting
That moonlight brings,
Bedecks their outer reaches.
While certain shafts
Penetrate the foliage
Unto the very heart of the beast.

At this time of day,
Yet dependent on the season
Almost another realm
Can appear to exist,
Merely fingertips from the one
That we perceive and hold as real.

Behold the Lord,
From a darker kingdom,
Takes form overhead,
The branches twist and shiver
At His will and passing
Upon His promenade and vigil.

Richard Gould

INTRUDER

What strange sense had wakened me so suddenly
I did not know.
Only that I lay instantly vigilant
In the sheet-grey light of that particular autumn dawn,
Waiting.

I heard it then.
A shifting of the frost-edged leaves
Disturbed uneasily from icy sleep.
Footsteps stirring the old stones.
Pausing
Very close now,
Stopping.

Barefoot-quiet I creep to the curtains.
Paler light slides in through the
Knife-like slit in the red velvet as
I put my eye to the edge.

A deer
Dark smudge soft against the frosty field
Stares back. Startled into stillness.
Transfixed in each other's worlds
We comprehend in that frozen moment
The force of fear.
Something unspoken passes between us
And is gone
As the deer bounds tracelessly away
Over the white grass.

Midge Bainbridge

THE BIRCH FOREST

Behold the shadow's solemn dance,
That mirrors the frantic flicker
Among birches bright and drench of moss,
A bounce of light graces the yellow archangels
That carpet the spindle feet of these bright pioneers,
Lords and ladies bow their still proud heads
To the regal spread, the insect banquet;
The earthy meal of bloated puffball;
The feast denied the skulking stinkhorn
And the reap of nefarious death cap.

Witches still fear this glaring army;
And the birch still protects the horse's mane
From the tangling fingers of the fairy
As they too are cast aside by the rising sun,
Heralded by a wild garlic wind
That whistles through teetering, flute-like trunks
And past the drum of the woodpecker's beak,
To tantalise the delicate bodies
That shy and desperately slither
Under bracken thicket or crumbling boulder.

Behold the refraction of life
Leaping from glistening webs;
Life will crack these brittle twigs,
Peer out from the blackened depths
Of this heavenly haven, this trembling refuge,
And insect legions will appear as one
To savour twilight's sorry death
As the all-immersing sun rains down,
Throwing a thousand shafts of dusty light
Through the emerald enchantment, the shimmering white.

Stephen Isaac

MOTHER NATURE

The elemental changes
Of Mother Nature
Are diverse and complete.
It is great to watch a storm
From the comfort of your room,
The sounds take you back
To being in the womb.
Thunder, lightning
Rain and snow.
They all make you
Want to go
Into a warm room
With a fire blazing.
Isn't it amazing?
Lazing about
With your animals
In warm clothes.
The socks on your feet
Warm your toes.
Mother Nature is great
She is wonderful.
Pray to her often,
She'll love you tenfold.

Maxene Huntley

WHERE DO THE SEAGULLS SLEEP?

When the sea, calm as a millpond
Seems to stretch forever
Before it reaches the sky,
You can scarcely see the join.
No wind on the turning tide,
All is a delight to the eye.
'Where do the seagulls sleep?'
Breaks into my reverie
Diving and swooping all day
They need some rest I agree.
I could see the lad's point
I didn't know what to say.
Expectant small face upturned,
'Where do the seagulls sleep?'
Must I betray my ignorance?
He knows when I play for time.
Watching the face of innocence
I think it is story time.
'When the light begins to fade
On the sea, all the seagulls . . .
Oh dear is that the time?
We must get home for tea.'

Betty Gilman

ON THE BANK OF THE WYE

That I should share this beauty,
Is more than I deserve;
To watch the surging waters,
Splashing, swirling as they wash
Over and around the anchored rocks.

Oh, that I were such a rock
Firmly embedded against the tide
Of life's many ups and downs
Strong in the Lord, and naught
To hide from or fear;
Washed and cleansed in
The river of His love.

Jean McPherson

DINNER TIME THOUGHTS

In leafy glade in summer's shade
with tablecloth and picnic basket
and chicken sandwiches to eat.
By hollow riverbed watching ducks
quack and flap their wings in
watery wake, while elegant swans
gliding by with beautiful plumage.
In the distance there are factories with
chimney fumes and people scurrying
by dinner time or to homes and
back to factory's macabre monotonous
chore, while workers with overalls
work at lathes and machines on
factory floor. Then five o'clock
buzzer goes and to factory gates
you go to walk or bike or car or
ride on factory bus back home you go.

R Law

THE MAGIC OF THE PURBECK HILLS

Potter back, to ever-enchanting Purbecks
With many sights and sounds before you.
An array of great unseen beauty, it demands respect:
Which I frequently review,
Where I stop and ponder a little
At the cool breeze so close to the sea;
With all the lovely wild flowers growing high on the leas
And to hear the high-pitched noise of the seagull's cry
Up high above in an overcast sky.
Most of the grassy paths do extend to the cliffs so serene.
The big yew trees are leaning against the Purbeck stone walls
So, up in ever-rising hill is an obliquity of dew
It is magic! and it will always be there for you!

Michael Davis

LOCUSTS

They appeared upon the horizon
As a billowing cloud,
Visibly pondering:
Hunger moistening
Their tiny jaws,
Indecision filling their minds.
Who should suffer,
Who was to have their crops despoiled?
They hovered upon the verge
Of hard-worked fields,
Curiously puzzling -
Their heads at work,
Making a choice.
Should they divide their swarm, or swoop
With a deathly humming
And envelope the plants like a shroud?

But not for them, these primitive scavengers,
Not the fine food of the field,
For like cannibals
They turn upon each other
And settle their small dispute.

Martin Winbolt-Lewis

PRECIOUS TIMES

The sweet perfume of ink-blotted bluebell wood
or buttered cowslipped fields.
Of sheltering in hollow oak
securely safe from drenching rain
emerging 'neath rainbowed sky
to wander home through leafy lane
sweet memories that remain.

To sit silent watching bustling stream
smoothing pebbles grey
while silver shadowed sticklebacks dart by.
Of lying 'gainst sateened musky hay
beneath a blazing sun
to gather first primrose or violet bouquet.

Seasonal displays cuddled close
when the day is done
opened comforting in time
treasured memories everyone.

Anne Edgar-Walters

EVERY WAVE

Will it be an ocean, come tide,
That is lost before
The rolling waves forget their cost,
To splash out inside,
Their midst acclaim.
The sea is swept with falling rain,
Onwards and through
Each, every wave sent
Comes splashing around us
To evade, circumvent,
Each life of its own
Splashes surf at will
And tide, after, gave
In its ebb ever still.
Sea creatures abandon,
They drift with the tide,
Their life long in swim cast
To be there set to hide
Midst all the seabeds
'Neath the coral's apt life
All so dependant,
On each other through strife.
Each needs the other.
We all need them all.
Some fierce or less timid
In their sealife recall.

Hugh Campbell

SEPTEMBER

Nights draw in
And lovely summer days
Are just a memory;
A treasured 'used to be'
Of time long gone.

Cool winds blow
And bring a hint
Of stark austerity,
Of winter 'yet to be',
Of summer flown.

September,
Her entrance decked
In summer's glowing fantasy
Of times that pleasure me.
Her days are short.

Frost bites hard.
Her exit's marred
By winter's cruel trampling
And all I long to see's
Reduced to naught.

H Strangwige

YAHWEH'S WONDERFUL CREATION

As the sun shines on a beautiful day,
As the birds sing among the trees.
As the grasshoppers hop among the grass.
As the monkeys swing from branch to branch.
As the branches flow from side to side.
As plants grow healthy and strong.
As the rain falls to the ground.
As you see the sun go down,
(What a beautiful sight!)
As you see the stars twinkle in the sky.
As you see a ray of light
Coming from the moon.
As you see thunder and lightning
Coming from the heavens.
(What an awesome sight!)
Remember Yahweh made it all:
Yahweh the almighty,
Made it all.

Miriam Elizabeth Black

LIFE SPRINGS ETERNAL

In the rising of the phoenix
From the ashes of the fire
New life springs eternal.
Sparkling like the dew
On a new day, a new dawn.
Life-giving,
Born of the new day, the butterfly emerges
From its time capsule of death,
To drink of the dew.
It spreads its wings in the warmth of the sun,
To rise triumphant into the sky, reborn.
Like the phoenix from the ashes
Free to live once more.

May Strike

NATURE'S CUSTOMER

What makes nature special to me,
Is so much, I am amazed.
Nature has so much wonders
I am so impressed.

I wake up at dawn
To the humming of birds.
Their early morning songs
Make me feel human.

As morning rises
I see the blue skies.
I go out in my jogging outfit,
And feel the fresh breeze,
The morning clean air.

I am so active,
In regular morning watch,
Of fresh breeze
I run into the Savannah forests.

The birds are graceful,
They fly with me,
I have become nature's customer
And so, they fly with me
As I take my early morning jog,
In magnificent morning rise
Of the spectacular sunshine.

Zaynab Armstrong-Jones

LITTLE PIDGE FINDS HIS VOICE

Hoorah! Hoorah!
Little Pidge has found his voice,
'Squawk, squeak, and squawk.'
He sits surveying Market Street from his three-storeys-up nest.
Just two weeks old, scrawny feather and downy fluff
Pidge in the flower box with the other egg that has not been hatched.
His bed a dried-up flower planter on the window ledge
of the town's bookshop.
Eyes bright, listening to the shoppers and the traffic,
Alone until Mam or is it Dad comes with a gullet full of food.
Pidge nestles up to Mam or Dad who is a wayward, ringed, racing
pigeon, not minding the May morning shower of rain.
Watching the famous 'Noir Blanco' - the great ridge tile walker
(alias pied wagtail to you and me)
'See the death-defying Noir Blanco - fearless in his pursuit of
excellence - no ridge tile too high or too long.'
Pidge watches then lies back down with eyes heavy in sleep, listening
to his lullaby of street voices - a woman's high laugh, a baby's
whinging cry, and the clock chiming the half hour.
The rain drizzling down making the street clean and shiny,
The dark dry earth and dried-up stalks of old bedding plants make
good camouflage for Pidge.
Mam or is it Dad flies off and Pidge sleeps - He is content on his own
with his would-be brother or sister egg to cuddle.
He is happy - he is loved
Mam or Dad is never far away - cooing occasionally from the butcher's
shop roof just across the street.
Mam or is it Dad arrives bringing more food.
Pidge squawks a greeting - then puts his beak into the throat of his
parent to take the regurgitated food, yum-yum!
It must be good for Pidge has grown on the town's leavings,
gleaned from wherever
A culinary surprise indeed for infant Pidge.
He gets up and flexes his wings
Tall, lanky legs, he looks so comical
He tries preening his feathers but gives up and shakes himself nearly

out of his nest.
He peers cautiously over the edge of the flower planter onto his street below
A strange set up - to be observed, being peered at from the occupants of the bookshop.
Quite the celebrity
Our little Pidge.

Hilary Jean Clark

ROSES IN JUNE

A broken spirit and a contrite heart
    God will not despise.
Her tears drowned her soul and her echoing cries filled the air,
    yet not a sound was heard.
Her sobs wracked her body and could not escape -
    they were locked inside the ever-closed doors to her heart.
Her favourite melodies rang in her ears,
    yet remained unheard.
Her laughter rippled like a stream but could not flow.
    Her words, her sentences of sadness and joy were carried off
    by the howling of the wind and were blown away
till not a sound of wind could be heard -
the wind had become a whisper.
Her secret prayers filled her room at night, as she talked to her one and
    only friend, her Lord Jesus, in the unseen world around her.
A bird in a gilded cage - which was now beginning to rust from age -
    there was no escape - for the door was locked and the key could
    not be found.
How she yearned to spread her wings and fly once more -
through the trees, the woods, the hills, around the flowers,
watching the sunlight, the moon and stars in the sky.
How she longed to be free - as free as the wind that blew through her
hair as she wearily walked around,
for winter was now drawing nigh,
    but in her heart a memory remained forever,
her summer and her roses in June.

Nicky Young

NOVEMBER METAMORPHOSIS

Now the greyness has been changed to silver,
An enchantment has come to November,
Mists are here, pale as powdered pearls bathing
The dark earth in dew that shines like embers -

From fragmented rainbows. The tufted lawns,
Rough and unkept glow with watery fire,
The spiders' webs are changed to crystal strands,
And the oaks from solidness retire.

In the fields, mist like a cloud counterpane
Hovers between last summer's dying grass
And the opaque rose-tinted winter sky.
A stillness reigns that hushes each bird's cry.

Misty alchemy, grey turned to silver,
Shining November metamorphosis.

Margaret Hibbert

ONE JANUARY AFTERNOON

The sky was aflame
That late afternoon:
Fierce - flaming, fiery-red,
In the western, cloud-filled,
Winter-seasoned, January sky:
So high, so high, so very high,
Full heaven-high,
Above my head.

And as I gazed in awesome wonder,
Each single, separate, leaping,
Twisting tongue of fire,
Each glowing ember, it appeared,
That had given such a daring,
Dazzling, and delightful display -
Was extinguished.
Slow at first, then swifter still,
As deep-black darkness overtook,
And each one disappeared.

Though nothing lasts forever,
Yet, it did seem,
That all that I had witnessed,
Albeit far too brief, was -
But an infinitesimal part
Of Creation's wondrous beauty -
And neither vision,
Nor a dream.

Glan Grey-Jones

WEATHERWISE

Snow-covered paddocks where Tack barn proud
invitingly prominent where donkeys stand
red hawthorn berries cling to hedgerow tall
while rabbits romp cleverly
avoiding us all.

Deer jump through fences as from window we stare
not daring to move while deer are there
blue tits hover from tree to tree
to peck at the nuts that are hung
especially for these.

There is holly in the hedges
and mistletoe on an old apple tree
there are fir and oak trees
ash willow and lime
and herbs a plenty such as
oregano mint sage and thyme.

There is a red brick house
with tiles that span
around its girth
higher than man
it is a house to look up to
yet not on a hill
where the welcome that greets one
is like the warmth of the sun.

Alas the folk are leaving for another domain
to leave us with memories again and again.

Hazel Sheppard

GLOBAL WARMING

Global warming
Now very much talked about
Seasons changing
Much conversation to flout

In the tropics where I was born
Lovely tropical weather making one cosy and warm
Many exotic fruit are grown
Many memories of life outdoors on a small farm

A world where people, animal and insects live
On this earth and in the atmosphere
Attention to quality of lives we must give
Because life is precious, therefore we must take good care

Care to reduce pollution
To make our world a safer place
Helping to reduce emission
Appreciate knowledge about how best to make this world a safer place.

Olive May McIntosh-Stedman

TO A HEDGEHOG

I saw you in the early light,
I did not hear your cry of pain,
Nor the roar of the vehicle as it passed,
But I found you dead in the morning,
Dawn forage, with sudden end;
Hunger pangs unsatisfied.

Gentle, timid creature,
Why should your end be so violent?
Where are your siblings now?
Do they await your return?

Could I but tell them, that
Taken from the lonely, exposed place,
You rest among the flowers,
In a garden paradise.

Joan Thompson

THE SONG IN US

After rain at night,
In the cool dawn,
See the raindrops hang
On the crisp leaves
Of the hand-shaped, wavy hedge.
As strengthens daylight
In cloud-wisped sky is born
A slow wonder - as if a bell rang
Or we stood on an awesome edge -
At what nature achieves
In small perfections as well as in stormy might,
Tempest, mountain, forlorn
Precipice, ocean and earthquaking pang
In all it conceives.
Between past and present drives a wedge,
We say - but -
Past is present in nature,
Yet there is slow, adaptive change.
Present, we say, is more mature
As we try to forget what might not arrange
Thoughts and instincts still wholly strong -

For whatever we become -
And that, at times, looks strange
And efficient and unlovesome -
Yet shall we ever be within range
Of nature's ambience - or we'll lose the song in us.

S V Batten

LITTLE WREN

Busy little wren minding your own,
Industriously occupying
Every minute of your daylight bliss
With efforts made and tasks fulfilled
So nothing's left amiss.
How can you find the time to sing
Being such a little thing as this?

David R Lucas

HALCYON DAYS

The rose-tinted glasses of youth,
of walking for miles in the sun,
lying in a meadow on warm grass,
listening to the village clock strike
and the distant sound of a tractor
as it circles an unseen field.
Not a cloud in the sky,
the only movement to be seen,
animals grazing quietly, or roaming
to another part of the field.
The sudden barking of a dog
as it sees a stranger passing,
looking down over the village
and wishing life could always be
so perfect and so peaceful.

A Odger

JOURNEYING THROUGH TIME

Birdsong awoke my sleepy slumber,
From this winter sleep of mine,
Subtle echoing, exchanging notes so clear,
Rhythmic, a melody's seer.

Conveying instant recognition,
Could this be the call of time?
When nature responds with the call of spring,
Highlighting source of growth, stimulating everything.

We have travelled so far this winter,
High over land, and many seas,
Having scanned snow and ice, o'er mountain peaks,
Creations glaciers of blue, historic value seeks.
Journeyed many miles over land, admiring magnificent views,
Amazed at the combination of colour,
Eagerly complementing each early morning dew.
Relishing the warm sun through time zones,
Relaxed, savoured, and condoned,
Pondered our awareness, over night and day,
Experienced nature's elements, obeying time delay.

But to hear the sweet birds in our garden,
Whether it be springtime, night or day,
For us it's a paradise of our making,
To be home once again in England,
One simply has to convey,
Fond memories we have of other places,
Amongst treasured family and friends,
We would rather stay . . .

Lorna Tippett

A Rusting Gate With Hidden Depths

I found you there one summer's night
Rustling and alone enveloped in ivy and columbine
Immovable yet with your rotting frame
But standing firm against attack
Plant life too, spiking - drawing blood
Attempting to deter.

Slowly you yield as I inch into your forbidden world
Things, shapes and substance take form
Covered and partly submerged by the
Force of nature when time stands still.
Your paths untrod and lost in a labyrinth
Of weeds and tumble briars.
Delight revealed, admired by none, but
Cover yet for animal and fowl.

Should I then disturb your tranquillity
Open up your quiet beauty and take
Faltering steps amongst your tumbling
Briars and cascading waterfalls.
Or come upon a night and sigh with the
Wind amongst your branches.
And lie on the moss unseen and revel with
You in your forgotten solitude.

Doris Hoole

SO WHO?

I have no belief in a God.
So who created the beauty of flowers
and
who thought of a rainbow after
April showers?

I have no belief in a God.
So who created the pleasure we have
from the warmth of the sun
and
what about the splendour and majesty of
a horse as it breaks into a canter
and begins to run?

I have no belief in a God.
So who created the joy we feel when
we see young lambs frolic and play
and
when we see the beauty of the countryside
as it shimmers on a hot summer's day?

I have no belief in a God.
So who created birds to fly
and to sing
and
why is it such a comforting feeling
to hear church bells ring?

I have no belief in a God.
So who created this world?
It wasn't me
and
I know it wasn't you.
So who?

D J Sim

WINTER'S WAR - LOST

Into that colourless, darkly brooding, tomb of winter
That which stifles and supplants the human spirit
With feelings of angst, animosity and aggression.

Into the shrieking pylon'd wires, sagging
Staggering 'cross puddled fields
Into the stark, leafless, rain-swept trees
Into the swirling brown tumult of burst'd rivers
Into the angry mountainous seas, whose
Beaching waves, consume the shore
Into these, the bastions of winter's reign
Slowly dawns the 'Phoenix Sun' of spring.

Slow-kissing horizon's silhouette lip
Forming her shapely swells and dips
Peeling away, black blankets of smothering nights
Exposing the wintered body, to a warm caress of light
Whispering urgent new promises among naked trees
Bedecking them with silvered green and budding leaves
The organic stimulation climbing to a peak
As the cold grip of winter becomes softened and weak.

Blue painted skies, flushed pink, appear
Dripping kaleidoscope colours into the young and fertile year
Eager birds chorus their sweet-clear anthem to spring
And winter's sterile shadows of war are once more - lost again.

Mike Pannell

HOME

No matter what the
Weather, even if it
Rains down, blazes
Boiling or snows cold
Blizzards all day long,
I'll be home. No
Matter what happens
Travelling home, I'll
Avoid harm, accident
And incident to
Come home. No matter
What my work, how
Weary I am, how hard
My day's been: I'll
Always be home.
Stay strong when I'm
Gone. Be good to
Yourself: fear not the
World, take heed from
Here. I'll be home.

Martin D W Clarke

SUMMER NIGHTS

As a bright sunny day fades away
and night begins to fall
little birds have gone to sleep in their nest
having sung all day
now it is the time for a rest
far above the velvet sky
a moonbeam is shining bright
stars twinkle everywhere
there is a whispering from the trees
gentle swaying in the summer breeze
hushed is the night
soon the stillness fades away
the birds begin to sing at dawn
and a new day is born.

Helene Birch

GUST

The prevailing wind is from the west,
On this south east coast,
Changing with the incoming tide.

Wind from the south produces heat in summer
And rain when you do not want it at all.

With the north wind comes cold, snow and birds
Flying south, stopping off for a while.

When the east wind blows sand is transported
In from faraway lands.

A south east wind pushes cloud out to sea,
Leaving the land as dry as can be.

October brings strong winds,
Moving leaves, branches, trees and electricity
Lines and poles, along with high waves
Beating against the sea walls.

G F Snook

SILENT HOUR

The silent hour of the early morn
When sleeping birds awake, anew
To watch the sunrise, reborn
And take its place in the sky so blue
Is to see the hour of green tranquillity
Shining bright and clean
Bringing a day of hope and peace
Whose tribulations are, as yet, unseen.
The silent hour of the early morn
Is when the colours of night disappear
Daybreak comes, charged with life
In the land that I hold dear
The greens and blues, and other hues
Still bedecked with the early morning dew
Portray a beauty only intended
For the eyes of a very few
Because this early morning peace
That each summer day is reborn
Can only be seen by the early riser
In the silent hour of the early morn.

Margaret Gurney

THE LATEST ARRIVAL

Before her, three figures appear
at the time each is expected -
yet somehow different -
less themselves then they were last year,
vague, not as warmly-rounded,
rainswept - and with less scent.

July grey, August overcast.
September steps in, seeks a shy
and somewhat withdrawn sun;
At last, urges wind to race fast,
fling the cloud - formation nearby
over the horizon.

So, the way scoured for October,
last to arrive here - and glowing -
a presence to inspire.
Swallows nearest to her remember
where earth's atmosphere is flowing
lit by star or sun fire.

She will overlook the harvest,
orange-gold flowers in her hair,
fruit baskets at her feet.
She knows where berries ripen best,
where fungi will erupt elsewhere -
she bites an apple sweet.

For her trees strew a leaf carpet.
The woodland turns from gold to brown.
For now, her skies are blue,
warmer than the summer - but yet -
how long before the rain slants down
and we bid her adieu?

Chris Creedon

WHEN THE WIND BLOWS

The trees sway this way and that.
The wind is as an orchestra.
The trees perform a ballet de Danse.
Slow and gentle, or frantic -
as the 'music' takes them - entirely at its command.

People, out and about, in the street,
Are trying hard, to keep on their feet -
Hunched forward, reaching out for some support,
To stop them taking to the air.

Leaves flutter across the sky
Round and round they go, spiralling upwards,
Taking all the dust, paper and other objects along
On a flying spree -
Before gravity deposits them, in some other destiny.

More leaves- green, yellow, red and brown
Scatter all around the town.
Pitter, patter, pitter, patter, raindrops add their subtle clatter.
Several umbrellas escape to join the dance!

Suddenly the wind drops, the 'music' stops,
All is silence and calm.
A wonderful experience of nature's beauty at play -
For the watchful observer - a wonderful day!

M Fitzpatrick-Jones

THE MOON

O, mysterious moon, which shines in the sky
When all on earth's surface is night,
The wise of the ages have sought to descry
The meaning of its wondrous light.

Astrologers thought it held secrets of days
Still far in the future to come,
And travellers have blessed its beneficent rays
To guide weary wanderers home.

The tides ebb and flow, and the months we can trace
As it waxes and wanes in the sky,
And to children its surface seems just like a face,
As the man in the moon they descry.

And when, sadly, the reason departs from the mind,
Superstition has sought for the cause,
And labelled men 'moonstruck' till scholars divined
The working of nature's great laws.

And now, not content just to gaze at the moon
And ponder its mystery in awe,
Man aspires to reach it, and so he has gone
Where the boldest ne'er ventured before.

But what of the problems that still here below
Call for urgent attention today?
Could the man in the moon only speak to us now,
'You are moonstruck yourselves,' he might say.

'Just look at the way you're exploiting the globe,
And at poverty, hunger and war.
You need not in regions far distant to probe,
For the lunacy's just where you are.'

John W Garland

PLANT WISDOM

The Sage grows like the humble moss -
Low and slow.
He shuns the sun of fleeting fame,
And creeps upon enduring rock.
He thrives where shadows fall,
And winter bites.

The Fool grows like the sunflower -
Tall and rank.
He seeks acclaim with bold display,
And nods upon his hollow stem.
He dies when fortune fades,
And summer sets.

Philippa Adburgham

WOODLAND MAGIC

The woodland glade stands silent as the sun's hypnotic gleam
seeps through the trees,
The secrets that lie hidden in nature's palms start to appear
from beneath the hideaway
We're inside the heart of the forbidden forest where the animals sleep
Where the boughs sway in the warm summer's breeze with
care and delicacy
So soft and clean they dare not breathe for fear of interrupting the
dreaming cubs
The careful deer bathes under the golden sun whilst the bunnies
play gleefully
As the fox keeps watch over the young, striding proud and important
Into the heart of the magic

The trees hold spirit and are obeyed and trusted by all the
woodland creatures
Nymphs and pixies bound about the undergrowth sprinkling purple
dust in the night air
As fairies create dreams that are held tightly in the web of
the silver spider
The forest is silent. Silent and safe beneath the strong boughs
Memories are created and kept secret even when the moon's
splendour takes control
As magic flows with ecstasy between the lavish green of the trees
Into the heart of the magic

We're inside the heart of the forbidden forest where the magic
of the world is made
In the hushed atmosphere of the creatures that create warmth
In the safety of the woodland glade

Sharon Barnes

ALLOTMENTS

Into a world of your own,
Like being in another place.
Digging, digging, with all of your heart,
transported into Heaven.
Keeping your body in trim.
Hard work, but what a reward!
Setting seeds, creating food and flowers,
veg like you've never tasted before,
full of flavour.
Flowers so beautiful,
the joy of growing,
the thrill of creating
a thing of your own.
Taking in God's precious air,
Oh to be alone, all alone,
Just with nature, and the living, growing things.
Heart in the very plot.
Time turning into an amazing sight.
A second home, all year long.

Joy Bartelt

THE ORCHID

Slowly it unfolded, yielding its delicate flower
Pale - with maroon artistry beyond compare.
A bloom suspended on a slender stem.
Alone it stands by the window, looking towards the fountain
And deep pink begonias.
Shy of the sunlight, it hides its forked tongue from unsuspecting insects;
While with its five-winged petals it rests, gold centred in silence,
adding to the stillness of the room.

Whose hand has painted such a flower?
Surely no earthly hand!
But the one who knows about creation and who loves beauty -
An artist who paints the incomparable skies of evening and
of early dawn;
While man sleeps from the business of the day.

K M Baillie

STORM

Morning clear and sun is shining
Sky so blue it is untrue
A gentle breeze disturbs the trees.
Life goes on as any Sunday,
People walking with their pets.
I know what he'll be doing
This Sunday, after lunch.

Clouds are gathering in the west
Sun still shining overhead
Mild for time of year
Wind is rising, more than a breeze
Some raindrops fall, no alarm bells
Wind quite stiff now trees are swaying.
Some fencing rattles in the wind.
Lashing rain drives people, scurrying.

Howling winds, trees bent over
Wind so strong one large branch
Passing by, just like
Traffic looked so normal
A traffic jam. *Oh,* what has happened?
A tree uprooted crashed upon
The road. Wind still howling by, in terrifying
Gusts, rain lashing, all are soaked.

A crack of lightning, all is still
The power is off *Oh dear!* No lunch
Men come out to see the tree
The chain saw's needed I can see
But all we have is but a handsaw.
It does the job and so traffic
Is free to flow quite freely, once again.

Within the house only candle light
A torch with strip light is all
We have to see how very strange.
So after tea of sandwiches and chocolate
We all four creep upstairs
And have our wash-time in the
Torch light and off to bed. Oh
What a *strange, strange day!*

R Murray

SKYLARK DAYS

Sweet larks, heard ev'ry day in youth,
But not heard now, five years or more,
Their songs cascading from the air,
As ever up the larks would soar
We'd lay our backs in meadow's grass,
To count black dots against the blue,
Then listened as the chorus swelled,
To fill our ears with joy anew.

It seems our summers then were long,
It never rained or so it seemed
When glancing back across the years,
To skies so blue and grass so green.
In Heaven's realm the lark was king,
With sweetest song from every bird
That filled the air with sheer delight,
When such sweet song might still be heard.

But now it seems, the larks have gone,
For now the fields that once were theirs
Are sown with towns instead of crops,
And roads now grow like bindweed there.
But who am I to say what's right,
(Or who indeed, to say what's wrong)
But in the fields I know I miss,
The glory of the skylark's song.

John Whittock

REFLEXES OF AWAKEN NATURE

Vibrating eyes from the womb of the Earth
Lucid as crystal fountain
Glittering like the full moon
Through your white eyeballs
I see the road that leads to your soul
Nature's beauty framed in heavenly glass
Heart of rose
Tread where the grass is green
The budding flowers ripen where human hearts are free
It is the whispers of early morning sunrise
The fragrance of full-grown
Yearning for initiation into the First Portals.

Ernest N Onuoha

FLOWERS

Graceful daffodil dancing down breezes blown
Free of golden rays which entangle ivy, hedge row
In file marching over buttercup trail.

Mimosa pastel melted in the cauldron of July
Wasteland bestowed with wild profusion, wisteria
Mauve longing to embrace any climbing reflection
Spoken out in shaded nooks and crannies collected
By purple pansies all smiling at humid humour.

Laughing lobelia row together down banks of
Crimson poppy fields blotched by occasional
Dreaming butterflies.

Lilies flatten reflected pond tops as glass woven
Tapestry depicted by abstract imagined petunia
Gleeful of petals which defy wind in movement of
Twisted stem erect for colourful standing.

Roses spread as honey tasted sweet for suckling of
Perfume arrayed in streams of wild cornflower
Poking above meadows unfallow yet adorned by
Pearls.

Shadows beneath iris abound with peony pleasure
Dancing round stamen togetherness pollinated in
Hives awash with catacombs assembled in perfect
Symmetry.

The bumble hops with buzzing nectar to enjoin the
Golden blooms.

The thorn pieces blazing azure skies as border
Asters congregate in peaceful harmony going in
Song to be scattered on rafted toad spawn.

The berries swing with circular intention and
Arrange their selves round Maypole playing.

Sunrays turn the circle of photosynthesis by
Osmotic penetration freeing cells locked by
Keyhole sod.

Preparing buds accrue greenfly in multitude and
Swallowed by ladybirds which bedazzle red of
Pebble-dashed spots in black tulip water still,
And held by the constructed clematis sprayed in prickled holly.

D Ramsey

UPON THE PLACE BENEATH

Gentle rain falls on a warm spring evening
Caressing trees as their leaves unfold
A warm earthy smell assails the nostrils
Signs that Earth is ready to be
Reborn

Summer heat, sticky and unrelenting.
The shade of leafy trees brings welcome
Respite as lovers seek shadows to
Profess their love for one another.
The gentle stream nearby
Meanders.

Autumn rains shake leaves from the
Trees turned gold, amber, red in a
Profusion of colour. There is a
Bite in the air, cold in morning, then
Hot midday until the mists and fog of
Evening.

High winds, rain lashing, no gentleness
Now. Storms beat upon sea walls,
Pebbles hit the sea defences and scatter
Across roads as if crowds of unruly youths do
Battle.

Warnings are given of winter gales and
Storms, God help those at sea but
Please God help us as the rivers burst
Their banks. Unforgiving rain swells meandering
Streams and rivers until water levels flood the very
Homes.

Somewhere in the world the excess of
Rain would be welcomed.
Somewhere the rains could bring
Forth green shoots at last.
Here in our island homes, we survey our
Muddy devastation with quiet despair.

Hilary Moore

AUTUMN ON DOGWOOD
(To Claude Monet)

Wildfowl, ragwort, bogweed and Thyme,
Blown to four quarters,
Run ragged
Thrashed.
Clouds tossed on a backdropping mile,
Stuffed into a lake like cottonwool,
And given that winter's great anvil
Shall soon crash from the sky
To distemper in lies white
The late one's venture.
More timely now.
More rarely to pass.

Alan Murdoch

THE MOORS

The moorland
Is barren and desolate
Like how I'm feeling now
Empty
Stretching on forever
Into the distance of my mind
Far and beyond
Our innermost thoughts.
Without you
I feel like the moors
Bleak and empty.

J Rowley

THE BALCONY

Breathtaking
The view of this beautiful landscape,
The deep green of the trees, the swift running stream,
The fields, the rolling hills, the clear blue sky.
The denial.
The lie.
High-rises, traffic reaching for miles, grey tarmac roads,
Black smoke and pollution,
Breathtaking.

Mariama Amoah

MOTHER NATURE

The rolling clouds, the crashing thunder
The darkness of a winter's night
Lightning flashes light up a darkened sky
Sending weird shapes rushing to the earth below

The howling wind that in March blows
Winter's snow to cover the hills and dales
Laying a carpet of white, a picture of such beauty
That only Nature herself could create

The babbling brook that winds its way
Through the valleys below in search of the river
Rushes to join the sea on which tall ships sail
Just like life, the river has its ups and downs
As it twists and turns to meet Nature's challenge

A summer sun riding high in a clear blue sky
Brings warmth to those on the earth below
The silvery moon in the month of June
A starlit summer night, all part of Nature's show
These wonderful sights must make one wonder
Who created the wind, the snow, the rolling clouds
The flashing lights and the crashing thunder.

J C Griffin

Rain

I can't go out, I can't!
I mustn't get wet, not me
I'll shrivel and shrink,
Of that I'm sure.
I don't do rain,
It's not my cup of tea.

I can't go out, I can't!
I'll sink, not swim,
I'll drown for sure.
I breathe air, not water,
I'm a mammal, you see.
The rain is not for me.

I can't go out, I can't!
Not until it stops.
I'll watch it from my window,
I'm safe in here.
Soon the sun will shine
Then I'll go and play.

Annette Murphy

WEATHER

Above all things earthly
governing our lives
lies an immovable expanse
that encompasses our globe

unconquerable by man
but fickle natured
one day dragon
next day angel

unsettled
yet irresistible
glorious
yet inexcusable

its fractured ozone
yields motionless
while animal clusters
defy pain

because the power beyond machinery
that beautifies the scenery
so often
heals the shame

and yet the darkness
that becomes light
at times even cynical minds
spiritually awaken.

Grant Bayliss

JACK FROST FAREWELL

The last spring winds are breezing in
To bounce May blossom down the lane,
Before the summer sun begins
To make our lives seem whole again.

The winter's charms are fine when young,
But as the years advance with haste,
One wishes that the cold be gone,
Blame Father Time for change of taste.

Upon these days of calm and still,
Our aching joints and fleshy quivers,
Bring evil smiles to Frosty Jack,
His pure delight to see our shivers.

But poor old Jack will never know
The warmth in front of log fire's glow.
He never feels his belly sigh
As hot tomato soup goes by.

If I were he, I would be gone,
Before advancing summer sun
Should melt away his silvery cloak,
Bepuddle him, and that's no joke.

Be gone cold Jack, be gone.

C H Baker

HOW I SEE YOU

A lone tree in a field,
Distant from those around.
Your roots, though unseen,
Spread for miles underground.

You touch those,
You may be unaware,
But they feel your presence.

From spring to summer you bloom,
Your branches become full and green.
Autumn to winter, they shed.

A sorrow befalls,
This you hide and brave the coming winds,
For you know your strength inside
Will see you through.

As surely and steadfastly spring returns
Covering you with her bloom
And once again you branch out and still
You're unaware of those around that seek
Your shelter when life seems hard to bear.

L Fryer

FALLING IN THE SCENE

Beginning from the fall to rise
an equanimity of renewed thought
to replenish, falling in your scene
of unification it has the mind caught.

Seeping in drop by drop,
abounding the Earth in its spell
somewhere it rules, somewhere it bestows,
washing ashore unburdened tides as well.

A catharsis of meandering pathways
or calmness coming to the brink
Sometimes transparent, pure and lucid
beckoning to the spirit in quest for a drink.

A sensational bowing of all the living
meeting all good deeds on the pier
a sound, a splash, a hailstorm
fast-flowing it gathers two worlds in fear.

Samina Amjad

A SINGLE DROP OF RAIN

Talk of Wales
And you will hear
So many people complain
Of the weather in the valleys.
'It just has too much rain,'
You hear them say
Again and again.
They don't appreciate the gentle pattering
Against a windowpane
Tell them how green is your valley
They will groan, *'But it never knows when to stop.'*
Do people know or understand
That some countries are aching for a single drop
Just to quench their dry land,
Just to bathe in,
They are even gasping for a drink?
And so many of us think,
Next year, we'll go abroad for sure.
So many other countries endure
Roasting sunshine all year through
Their lands are dry to the bone.
And here so many people continue to groan
If only we could give some other countries a loan
Of a single drop of our rain,
Would it be enough to sustain them?
I know too much rain here is never wanted,
But we really shouldn't take rain for granted.

C A Keohane-Johnson

ALMIGHTY SEA

Oh rage of the sea, won't you listen to me
Stop pounding the rocks by the shore
Hold your almighty anger, be gentle and calm
Be the fisherman's friend, they don't do any harm.

Let the ships carry cargo from lands to and fro
So that all men who love you will envy you so
When you rant and you rage, you stir fear in their hearts
Then your gigantic waves just tear them apart.

Your vastness is great all over the world
Your time is forever, to have and to hold
But man has only a few years compared
To a never-ending sea, who clings to its fold.

You have claimed man and treasures
From eternity of time
May God in His wisdom hold forth His hand
He Himself holds the secret of the man and the sea
We have faith, we have love, you shall see.

V Day

THE RIVER

Meandering slowly on its course
Peaceful waters flowing by
Where it started? What's its source?
I ask the question, no reply.

The fish in the river swim upstream
Their tail fins swishing to and fro,
Bright sunlight on the water makes them gleam
In the clear water river flow.

Sitting here on the riverbank
Feeding the ducks with bread,
Nothing seems to bother me,
Perhaps it's all in my head!

Jeff Parks

BELOVED DAISY

A poem should open
   closing like a flower,
Yet another charming puzzle
   studied for hidden meaning
Surprises, intrigue to be life-like
   dream-like wonder
Thus the novelty in keeping
   fact or fiction?
Exploring truth or imagination
   vibrant floral kaleidoscope
There now cognisance endures
   instant, ironic, love blossoms
Enter beauty, original reflection defined
   self expression, emotion
Words of hope a kiss
   chasing away the tears.

Elsie Scrowther

THE LONELY HILLSIDE

Upon the lost and lonely hills,
I roam along that deserted path.
The sheep that bleat and birds that chirp,
Are sounding in my ears.

The sun-bright golden daffodils
Are reflecting on my clothes.
I like the little red roses
And the long purple heather too.

Along the path, step by step,
I'm surrounded by trees and plants.
As far as I look, I can't see anyone,
Only the birds and sheep for company.

Sunset's spreading over the sky
With its magical colours.
The sun-copper trees are shadowing
A lonely little stream.

Lisa Christie

MR BUMBLEBEE

I watched a bumblebee today,
He was rubbing his back and rubbing all around,
Only holding on with a couple of legs,
I thought he was going to fall to the ground.
But no, there he was going a-buzzing on his way,
What a lovely few minutes it made
To my almost boring day.

Marie Edwards

SHORE SONG

It hypnotises me,
This ocean lullaby.
It draws me into daydream
It sends me out beyond
And soothes away all need for thought,
All care for my tomorrow.

Andrew Hirst

NATURE

Nature is the master painter
He paints from the blush of the baby's cheek
To the fire in the grate at night
With his brush he blends the colours
As no other artist can
Just one glance in the fields
Will tell you what I mean
For who would put together
So many reds and greens
His moods change dramatically
Like all artists do.
From the dark nights
To sunny days
Where happiness shines through
The colour phases of his life
From winter white and summer blue
The gold and browns of autumn
And springs' many hues
With his palette and his brush
He paints the canvas
We call the world
And with our own greedy, foolish ways
His masterpiece we maim
We cut the rainforests
And with insecticide and sprays
Soon there will be no picture
Only the sun's rays.

Doreen Wilkinson

LOOK TO THE COUNTRYSIDE

Look to the countryside
Where the air is always clean,
Where there is always the notion
Of Nature's liberty,
Where one may find the surroundings
Which they need,
Yes, look to the countryside,
Where one may discover another land
That has been in their dreams,
Fields full of growth, brimming over,
With wheat and corn,
Also new cereal yields that give
The farmers the thought of showing
That they have produced something
That is making helpful contribution
For the world itself.
Yes, to them this is so real,
The countryside is a place where people
Need to be left alone, with thought
Of the animals to have a perfect home.
Yes, just look at the countryside
Where so much life is at bay and can go on
Showing that there is a Lord
In a higher place, who looks over it
From day to day.

C Hush

PELICAN

Diving Prehistoric for your silver shimmering prize,
Falling and ascending in the prehistoric skies
Tell me what's been witnessed with those ever-living eyes
What contents in the story of such prehistoric lives.

What can you be thinking, what has come before
Seeing toasting bodies laying on your shore
Soaring high above, planning precise to fall
Do you see the same as us, or now and then and more?

Emma Cantillion

OUR SURROUNDING WORLD

Crashing
Another wave at the rocks
Your silent seabed waits
The moon-graced ocean
We practice so often. Escape
To touch and grasp onto your reality
Plunge into your deeper realms
Breathing your arousal
Surreal in perfection
Rhapsody excites the tides
Wash me away with this lechery
Repeating over and through
From the dark nadir rushing
To elevate to our never-ending zenith
Close your eyes and escalate
Hazy naivety that calls
Lose your breath to catch
Those oracles of ousters
Rarity captured
In a lustre so unique
Turning beyond our dreams
Never looking back
Emerge the surface
Retreat to your aquatic beauty
Droplets of water fall from you
Submersed in the underworld
Infuse your pure sense of thought
Immune from drowning
We inhale each other's life
And continue to
Become
One existence.

Andrea M C Coleman

VI

Spring's coming through
and here's the blossom
to prove it

lighting up the reddish clay
and fatigued khaki
of the Sentmenat landscape,

sorbet-fresh,
snowflake-bright,
the cherry blossom

not quite pink,
the apple blossom,
not quite white,

but white petals washed
with a single coloured one -
a seed of pigment

forgotten in the drum -
and hung out to melt
on these taut, stretching branches

like the Earth's sigh
for chthonic truce:
winter's exhalation.

Daniel Davies

COCOON

Caressing to and fro her prey
Mother Black is watching, waiting;
her beady eyes bulge huge with pleasure
banqueting in her mind
on the slow-rounding lump of life
so sweetly entangled
enchanted now with heady odours,
and croons her lullaby.

Hush now, my pretty, and all will be well
Old Mother Black is casting her spell,
she'll keep you and guard you and wrap you up tight
and Old Mother Black will be happy tonight:

Warmth gently creeps over, softly
stealing all power of movement,
only rocking, rocking in the breeze
nothing left, for me, but sleep . . .

In the daybreak, broken threads hang
and a late owl hoots softly
at a rustling in the trees;
and somewhere, a spider is smiling.

Tia Thomson

PEREGRINATING MOON

Magical moon
in wingless flight,
lighting the paths and balconies
of timeless, sweet accord . . .

Moon continental,
lighting peaks of glistening parasols;
riffling fingers of light
through formless huddles of conifer;
reflecting signals of cordial lakes;
seeping through eyelids
closed on private dreams . . .

Voyager moon
mirrored in slumberous
swells of sleeping waters . . .

Rural moon
strobing playful badgers;
freezing, in sudden light,
the red fox near roosters' pens;
running sinuous, silvered streams
to pale outlines of distant coasts . . .

Sullen moon
in clouded purdah cast,
floating, unseen, on seas of stratus . . .

City moon
clothing spires and towers
in vestments of light and shade;
outraged by bawdy flashers of street neon;
catching the arcs of murderous knives
in dingy alleyways;
spreading milky balm
in gardens of quiet sanctuary . . .

Thespian moon
retiring through cirrus curtains
above the slumbering stage . . .

Homing moon
spent by the long night . . .
pallid to advancing sun . . .
deferring to The Steward of Day.

Ron Hails

WHEN THE WIND BLOWS

As the wind blows it sends
Messages from above,
The wind may be warm, cold
Or even freezing.
It sometimes dries your clothes,
It sometimes makes you
Wrap up nice and warm,
It sometimes brings relief,
So really speaking, the wind
Is in fact a friend.
It may bring a chill or even a thrill,
It brings sailors forward on the sea.
The wind, we are grateful
For thee.

Paula Natalie Turner

TORNADO

Woken!
By the taunts of the angry wind
Throwing hailed threats at my window;
Sending Levin fire-crackers
Reverberating around the sky.

The gauntlet is delivered
As a tornadic fist is driven through the glass.
The screams of delight spiral around me
As I, terrified for my life,
Bury my head
Beneath the impotent duvet.

Then silence.

Alive!
I peep from my shelter
To find my tormentor gone;
Leaving me staring
At the devastated space which had been
My bedroom wall.

Joy Morton

ILLUSION

A silken shawl of moonlight
Silvers the rural scene
Beneath its folds lies evil,
Wickedness unseen.

Serene perhaps by night and day
Appearances deceive
Cruelty and incest here
A watering-hole for thieves.

In the darkened church the vicar prays
Not for sustenance for his flock
But for anonymity
When he is defrocked.

In his cottage of thatch
Macho man sleeps
Soundly, without care
His wife bruised and bleeding
Wishes herself elsewhere.
How long can she endure this
Far better she were dead
Should she end it with the tablets
Or take a knife to him instead?

At the Manor House the parvenus
Count ill-gotten gains and gloat
Enemies won't find them here
So peaceful and remote.

Next time you see a village
A jewel of flowers and thatch
Consider what you might disclose
Should you dare to lift the latch.

Vera Morrill

A New Year, A New Beginning

Our new year began with the shining lights
Of the year now past.
Let's keep in our minds this memory -
Closing the door to misfortunes.
A little colour can be seen; one little
Camellia peeping through the centre
Of our heavily-laden shrub.
A few primroses gently blow in the icy breeze.
This is a promise that whatever happens,
Nature will do its best to assure us
That whatever the weather brings
Their faces will shine as brightly as
Our fairy lights.

Norma Pusey

WINTER RAIN

I touch the shadows in the window
    a divine source from above
The mirrors of the raindrops
    surround the alchemy of life.
Water is the healer of all life forces
    a transformational process.
The start of a new year, a new beginning.

Pam Bridgwater

YOU AUGUST

August rushed in like a mighty wind,
It showed off its sunshine through clouds,
Mist and rain, the height of summer
Warm sunshine should be,
But oh, how it fools one with games it does play!

The sun laughs as it breaks through the clouds,
Watching you mow the lawns, cutting down hedges,
You feel so relaxed in the sun and air,
But little do you know, the rain's creeping near.

As you gather up branches and sweep up the grass,
The sun's creeping out and the clouds rushing in.
So engrossed are you with the flowers,
Planning to sit in the deckchair with tea.

Unaware are you that the cloud's going to burst,
So the sun laughs behind the black sky and peeps;
Oh August! How could you play games and be so unkind?
You watch while the rain pelts down on the line.

No time to rescue the clothes on the line.
The mower, all wet, the cutters all rusting.
I know you, old sun - you are laughing up there,
Seeing us drenched to the skin, rain dripping from our hair.

Just as we manage to rush into the house,
The cloud rushes past and sun, you come out!
What is your game - do you think it's fun?
Well I feel, August, you need a good clout.

Rosina M Drury

FACING THE FALL

Wasps, deprived of picnic
Abandoned since the autumn dew-soaked grass,
Seek out the neighbouring orchards,
Burrowing greedily into fallen fruit.
Bees, lethargic in the cooler days
Make late forays into treasure chests
Of flowers plumping up their seed cases,
Or swelling rhizomes hidden underground.
A butterfly pirouettes in gentle breezes,
Seeking where to lay its eggs,
To perpetuate its brief hours of glory.
Flies insinuate themselves into houses,
Bumble around disturbed by lights,
Whilst house spiders spin endlessly
To catch the intruders for a future feast.
Plump woodlice too find sheltered corners,
Huddling in an armoured melee,
Jousting with the prongs of earwigs
For choicest refuge from the coming cold.
Fish no longer await the dancing mayfly,
Woodpecker's arousing rap scares few ants.
The creeping, crawling days of ended summer
Are now replaced by driven need of preparation
For the icy sleep of months to come.

Di Bagshawe

SUMMER

A season of memories,
All good.
Romance and love frame many thoughts.
Sporting heroes grow from the back streets of hardship.
Miracle songs last on eternally in everyone's minds.
The moon shows hard for the few hours relinquished by the sun.
Warmth always lingers haplessly on the backs of children.
For many those short few months last for years,
Even occasionally a lifetime.
Summer is always remembered.

Ian Fisher

NEW YEAR NOEL

That winter our family geese were stolen,
soundlessly at night, like drugged watchdogs.
Grandma and Grandpa grieved for the birds
they'd raised, and feted as celebrities, for Christmas.
We delayed displaying our presents until January.
At Grandma's, the tin bath was suspended opposite
a bacon flitch, work tools hanging upside down like bats.

Window frost imitated Grandma's crochet work,
Grandpa claimed, elbows on knees, squatting hearthside
on the dwarf, three-legged stool he'd carved from a
pit prop. His miner's boots yawned on their sides, studs
scintillating by firelight. His braces dangled behind
him, a parachute harness, I fancied. With clasp knife
he daintily peeled the apple from his collier's stocking.

In a solitary spiral it snaked to the flagstone floor.
We always applauded and encored him. Grandma
rolled her Bizet-Carmen eyes at Heaven, floury handprints
on her pinafore. Fresh bread fragrance contested the
painted, varnished toys our Da had secretly hand-made.
Magi status gifts: a soldiers' fort; a dolls' house,
matchbox furniture upholstered with Mam's recycled rags.

'Before long,' Grandpa prophesied, 'you'll only
be able to get toys from shops!' His gloom
was epiphany to us. Maybe in his mind
he was still chasing goose thieves.
Nothing ever surpassed Grandpa pantomime-peeling
his Yuletide apple in one magic coil.
But he never reared Christmas geese again!

Malcolm Williams

SPRING WILL COME

The lark will soon be singing above the downs,
The first daffodils be shooting up,
Blossom be in orchard,
The pale sun flowing over treeless hills;
And tomorrow we shall take
Familiar paths again.
But who would know
That man, this moment, is firing six-inch shells,
Torpedoing merchantmen, bombing open towns,
In the name of peace slaying and being slain?
Yet soon I, like many others,
Will go reluctantly
And do the same.

Paul Gardner

SEPTEMBER SONG

Glorious September
Once more holds out
Her arms to greet us
Gone are the heady days
Of full summer
July's blowsy brashness
August's stark hot
Brazen abandon - departed!

Gentle, kind September
Is here again, with her
Soft warm tenderness
Crowning glory of the
Summer, herald of
Early autumn, easing
Our path slowly to
A quieter, more natural rhythm.

Generous September
Bringing Mother Nature's
Fruits into full maturity
Preparing to give so
Freely of herself
Offering up her bounty
To man's ready and
Eager touch.

Good September
Opening the doors to
A new beginning
For young people everywhere
Embracing all children
In her reassuring arms
As they move expectantly
Into a new school year.

Give thanks once more
For another perfect September
A secure bridge between
Summer and autumn
Let her take you by
The hand and lead you
Forward - she will
Never disappoint you!

Barbara Manning

ANOTHER NEW YEAR

Just think ahead to the spring, then summer
Autumn followed by yet another winter
And it all starts again, 365 more days
In January the mornings are frosty, ground covered in a glaze.

By March we have the winds, April showers, often
Pellets of hail, pounding on the pavements,
Then comes along May, with blossoming trees,
Their pastel flowers prettily marking out avenues and lanes.

Along comes summer, with its hazy sun and hot days,
We look forward to those, no coats to weigh us down,
A long cool drink just an arm's length away,
Long days full of light in June, July and August.

September and October are back,
Swiftly autumn creeps up, the colours of the leaves change
To bronze, burnt orange, even yellow or red, suddenly
All is stark, dull and the green has disappeared, once more
November and December are approaching.

Our year has passed, so quickly
We've almost missed it. Where have all those days gone?
The clock has sprung forward one hour,
Then fallen back, one hour.

We search for what we felt was lost
As if it had been hidden, or we'd mislaid a precious item.
If only we had realised that it wasn't missing at all,
We *had it all the time!*

L White

WINTER CHILL

Winter chill returns
And the trees motionless, thrust their gaunt features skyward,
Just as they always do.
Just as they did last year and the year before that.
Back to my grandfather's time!

A brave glimpse of green was it, that dared to peep
Beneath frost's gentle drapery,
Or did I imagine it was real,
Drawn from some last year's memory?

Now where an icy trickle once was raging water,
Kate comes dancing. Singing and dancing.
Singing her merry song of youth
To fill the earth with summer gladness
I can only dream of.

Soon, winter will be just another memory.
And as long as I can remember
And my father before me
And his father before him,
It will always be so.

S Joyce

UNDERNEATH THE APPLE TREE

I said, 'Good morning, summer,'
because summer sparkles, doesn't it?
Oh, doesn't it just

an early riser certainly wears it well
as he or she falls from my gaze but they join me
in a feast of heavenly grandeur

the air is bustling with silence
as the sun hits through branches
and there is wispy white
but mostly benevolent blue

my bare feet tickle
as a brave wee breeze pushes through
causing gangly green to tease between my toes
but my eyes and mind are not at ground level

my horizons show a tractor
working as slow as the day suggests
and a boy at a burn throwing stones
in his own little world

when a dog barks life decides to show itself
as birds scatter in a panic
and I return from a pleasant dream

rabbits pop up, ears propped
looking for danger but yet all they find
is a day worth more than their worry

strawberry jam rolls for me at tea
and bread for the birds as colours emerge
pass and leave us for another day

nightfall creeps in, stars set up

badgers and foxes go out
while I run down
I'm two hours late

Cameron McAulay

WINTER FEELINGS

Winter sunlight shining through the buildings
Warming my heart because we are together
Like children running and laughing in the city
Aware that this is the most precious time of all

The river running to the sea
Takes all our sadness with it
At the start of a new millennium
Our hearts may start to feel love and joy again

I never thought that it would be like this again
Suddenly London is the most beautiful city in the world
Why? Because you are here with me at last
And wherever you are becomes beautiful to me

Together under wintry grey skies or storm clouds
My life will always be bright if you are there
Making my heart feel as if it will burst with joy
Making the old dark streets alive and colourful

Thank you for making my life special again
Where once it was going nowhere
Now bound on a course towards that special goal
Which we both want and need so much.

Phillipa Grundy

NAKED WINTER

Naked winter bears now down
Upon all the land.
Its icy fingers shrivelling and burning
Everything with cold fire.
All nature cowers in its presence.

Even the distant moon shudders,
In gleaming, cold response.
Water dies an icy death and ripples not,
Jack Frost has his frozen heyday,
Giving things his scorching footprints.
Oh the spring, the spring,
Will it never come?

K I Squires

WINTER NIGHT

Out of the door from the close dark room and feeble lamps
I stepped into a new and open world.
A white sheet puffed with frost clung icily to the line
I stood arms poised to take it down and then looked up

To see the silent clarity, sheer cold and sparkle of the winter night
Moonlight struck sharply the shivering trees
Stretching to the skyline in a delicate dance of silvered heads
All around and above a crystalled hedge.

Away and high swung the sky, aeons distant yet sweet, near and sweet
As the frost in my mouth, and in my throat its Nordic midnight blue
Sang so loud it stopped my breath.

Swirling canopies of distant sky moved over my head
Too free, too rare, over-dazzling senses and mind.
I ran and ran into the warm and sheltering house, but remember still
The stars, the cold, the music of that moonlit winter night.

Sylvia Fairclough

WINTER

Soulless and sad, winter
Shrouded in an aching grief,
Deprived of survival and light,
A season in mourning.

Biting winds sweep the landscape,
Branches stripped bare, creak in distress.
Desperate for shelter, sheep huddle
In woolly packs, 'neath a sombre sky.

Clothed in silver frost, fields lie barren,
Awaiting the warmth of a newborn life.
In the distance, the sweet warble
Of a robin, unites harmony with hope.

Juicy berries deck the hawthorn,
A festive feast for hungry birds.
Light fades, haunting shadows loom
In the moonlight, the close of day.

Through the farmhouse window, a lantern
Sheds a warm, welcoming glow.
Snuggled beside the fireside, a family
Raise their glasses to the season ahead.

Diana Frewin

SPRING

Robins, blue tits and blackbirds
Come into the garden,
Feeding from the bird nut containers
Flitting back and forth in the trees,
Tweeting and singing their song.
The occasional frog jumping around,
Worms and snails visiting too.

The winter plants shrivelled by the frost,
Waiting for the warmer sun to liven them up,
All the pretty spring colours
Of mauve, purple and yellow,
To brighten everything up.
Daffodils, pansies and crocuses
Flapping in the spring winds.

Rosemary Tester

JOYS OF SPRING

Loving spring
As we do,
Watching flowers
Coming through.
Buds and petals,
Green and hue,
Bunnies hopping
All around,
Lambs springing
On the ground.
Sun comes shining
Through the skies,
Brightening up
All our lives.
Thanking God
For all He's done,
Making our lives
So full of fun.

Jennifer Williams

WINTER BOUND

The mist outside was grey, interminably grey.
Holly leaves crackled.
They were the only colour in the snow.
No cars, no sledges.
The moaning wind dropped.
All was still.

Where was the sound of children's voices,
The colourful hats and scarves?
I was trapped and frozen in the cottage
Even the sound of the holly leaves was life.

Wind, blow the snow from the hills
Break the icicles,
Make drifts on the empty roads.
Clear the mist that I may see,
Bring life to this frozen silence.

Jane England

SOMERSET

The snow fell in Bath today
and made the house-tops white.
Each little flake came tumbling down
and made a pretty sight.
If only you would stay awhile,
before you melt away,
I'd make a snowman
large and white,
where children go to play.

Tom Clarke

RAINY AUTUMN EVENING

Smell the burning leaves
smoke from the bonfire
hangs in the rain soaked air
hovering - a gentle ghost.
Raindrops on the windowpane
are transformed to diamonds
courtesy of the street lamp.
The fire glows in the grate,
filling the room with soft flickering light.
The heralding kettle's cheerful siren sounds.
Aroma of toast browning on the grill
wafts appetisingly by.
The twilight sky now turns dark.
Draw the curtains and dream of summer days.

Ivy Allpress

QUICKENING NEW LIFE

New springtime's quickening life
Reveals spring is everywhere
Glimpses of spring's gentle smiles
See how sunlight streams
Through tall trees
Warming springtime's wild fragrant flowers.
Dead oak leaves leap fast away
In spring's soft breeze
Revealing many new primroses that peep and creep
Among woodland's mystic scenes
How wonderful a view through March and April
The woods carpeted in yellow, white, purple anew.
No sound where spring flowers burst into bloom
Nor when a smile lights up the gloom
Visions clear
Flickering sunlight
Glamour's gleam
As springtime peeps out
From winter's lonely bare trees.

Pamela Hopes

The Thunderstorm

The night was so oppressive,
Before the storm began.
The sky so grey and impenetrable,
Awaiting the bang.

Suddenly it started,
A shaft of orange streaked the sky.
The storm becoming orchestrated,
The birds ceased to cry.

The thunder roared,
The lightning flashed,
The sky lit up once more,
Nature's might performing a wonderful score.

Sulphurous fumes
Hanging in the air,
An awesome scenario,
To behold everywhere.

Then suddenly silence,
Then peacefulness and calm,
We thankful in the aftermath,
The storm hadn't done much harm.

Molly-Ann Kean

THE LITTLE CHERRY TREE

On All Saints Day
They fell,
Forming a pool
Of golden clothes
Upon the grass.
No higher than a man
The little tree
Stood bravely,
Semi-naked.
The remnant leaves
Trembled
Upon the undeveloped limbs;
Valiant and vulnerable
It seemed,
Attempting adulthood,
Yet each thin branch
Betrayed the shy young girl.

Mary Waegner

OXFORD, WINTER 1962

Those were the days when it crossed our mad March minds
That Zernov might be glad for the first snow
And our philologist from Queensland freeze to death.
Time had closed an enigmatic eye
On the tough community of Sunday Russians,
Old grey heads and young heads sprouting plaits,
Nodding in prayer, chaste in the candlelight.
    (Remember when the censer slipped its chain
    And rolled like a celestial grenade
    Towards old Zernov, smoking at his feet?)
Time has not changed that pale ghost of a girl
Who ran like a bird to catch the falling snowflakes,
White and icy in the dazzling shadow
Of the multi-storey engineering block.
Still time is lingering in the libraries.
Essays evolve from great men's quiet asides.
Old books impart new wisdom to the wise
And young minds grasp the great uncertainties.
Time, it seems, turns ideals into ice.
Like snow our dreams have frozen perfectly.

Death may take life but not a way of life.
Ideals will go the way of thistledown
To multiply minutely in their dying.
It is a joy to know there's no outliving
A winking city merrily protecting
The bird-like girl
With graceful intellect and long dark hair,
The aquiline, undaunted predator
Of grey illusions,
The polyglot and chortling theologian,
The 'enfant terrible' and the dying don,
Zernov's world without end.

Jeremy York

PITIFUL DEFIANCE

The autumn rain falls
But my red geraniums
Bloom still,
Defiant towards the waning year.
Sad rivers of rain
Trickle through the cracks
In the paving slabs
Nourishing the roots of weeds
We pull in a senseless drive
To control wild nature
In this old garden
That has seen more seasons
Than we ever will.

Soon I will have to take up my flowers
And wrap the roots in warm compost,
Shelter them from vicious winds
Through endless days of winter grey
As I, and they, wait for the spring.

Through the streaked glass I see
The transient beauty of golden autumn
Moribund in the leaves on paths and verges.
The conkers have been collected
And all the trees can do is sigh
Giving up the last of their leaves
In tearful surrender
As the claws of winter
Slice bark and bough
Stripping them bare.

Jo Leak

STRAINED RELATIONS

Cold. Moonlight through the diamond panes
Floods on her gold, her silver and her jewels.
Sly, moonbeams splinter on his tinsels of success:
But it is shadowed where the true cost lies.

It is the slow nocturnal pat upon his back
That tells the truth beyond her, 'Never mind,'
And smiles that do not reach sad empty eyes
That watch the wall, and fill with tears.

It is the truth that cries, when silent pain
Corrodes the certainty, and doubt sets seed
To root in fertile ground. It is the truth that lies
With, 'Doesn't matter,' and her pat upon his back.

Alan Chesterfield

SNOW

Now I am falling crisp and white
To change the winter's scene
I cover bleak and barren land
And make it bright and clean

I fall upon the branches bare
And make them seem so pretty
The cold black trees I will transform
In countryside and city

I fall on roads and fields alike
So all are smooth and even
My white flakes fall so silently
To light the sombre season

The sun shines down from clear blue sky
Upon my cold white day
I gleam and glisten in his light
But soon I'll melt away

My fragile beauty cannot last
His rays are growing stronger
I feel my life is fading fast
I cannot stay much longer

Joan M Jones

WINTER

Winter;
an obsidian mirror at the
equinox of the year,
its crystal dark reflection
looks to spring
from the Orphean deep of autumn.

Bells cast of meteoric iron
ring clear in ice-cold clarity.
Even the Horae sleep.
Frozen ponds hold images of
a Narcissus who waits for the sun.

Persephone sleepwalks;
from her footsteps
the snowdrop and crocus spring as dreams.
Slowly, Hera winds her clock anew;
through fern-frosted glass
she sets the hands at midnight.

Phillip T Watson

THE AUTUMN LEAVES

The artist sits on the cold stone steps beside the grown-over dam
Then leans back to view his scene before bending over
To dip-and-mix the water colours to blend in exactly
With what he sees near to him and far to the west.

All takes shape and forms with each careful brushstroke
                                        delicately weighted
To deliver the correct depth of colour onto the pale paper.
Falling and fallen leaves cover broken tree limbs that are
Thrown towards ripe clusters of chestnuts autumn-after-autumn.

The scene fixes in the cold north wind that now plays with
                                        the helplessness
Of the artist's overturned water cup; it spins aimlessly
On its narrow, unbalanced, hollow-dented base, tapping
Its out-of-tune song on the well-worn village steps.

John Michael Doherty

THE WOODS IN WINTER
(... Here Lara stopped, closed her eyes and took a good breath of the air which carried all the smells of the huge countryside. It was dearer to her than her kin, better than a lover, wiser than a book. For a moment she rediscovered the meaning of her life ... Doctor Zhivago, Boris Pasternak)

The well-worn paths were as familiar to her
As her own reflection.
Usually she walked alone, picking her way
Over the pitted tracks of sand and stone.
It was one of those rare winter days
When the skies were clear and transparent.
As the sun began to sink its blinding rays
Flickered and flared between the dense lines
Of trunks in an explosion of light.
The skyline was flushed from gold to pink.
Across a barren landscape the silhouettes
Of an isolated group of trees reared
Like a charging cavalry frozen in flight.
Birds swept the emptiness in fluid shoals
With the graceful precision
Of biblical fishermen casting their nets.
She loved the woods with a passion
She did not try to define;
The forest opened its heart to her
And enfolded her in a warm embrace.
She turned into a wide grassy avenue,
An immense roofless cathedral, and walked
With a reverence as though towards a shrine.
Slowly the shapes around her melted into the dusk
And disappeared without trace.
She was drawn into this vortex of annihilation
So that she merged with every shadow and tree
And became as one with all that surrounded her.

A great peace entered her soul making her feel
Strangely disembodied and free.
She moved forwards into the gloom and the silence
And for a brief moment she understood
The meaning of life and of her own existence.

Rosina Winiarski

WINTER'S SHROUD

The morning mist hangs
Like damp blankets surrounding,
Obscuring the view.

The freezing dampness
Gnaws at body and senses
In the dumb stillness.

Shapes invisible
Wrapped tightly in thick billows
Till sun tugs them off.

Branches will sparkle,
Dewdrops become diamonds,
Gems of winter days.

Pat Heppel

WHEN THE WIND BLOWS

The cruel wind continues to blow my way
He serves to remind me of my insecurities
As he strips my roof, takes up the apple tree.
The cruel wind continues to blow my way
He serves to remind me of the winter.
The barren-winter that is riding on his tail coats
As he rat-tats at my back door
With all the civility of a gentleman caller.
Yet I know him as the wolfish, thrill seeker
Who only seeks to blow me and my house away.

N Daly

AUTUMN

The golden light illumines all,
This glorious autumn day,
The wind-blown trees like jewels wave,
Along the country way.
A magic world which casts a spell,
Enthralling all who see,
Cast off your fears,
Take on the cloak,
Of autumn's majesty!

Mary Hughes

SUBMISSIONS INVITED
SOMETHING FOR EVERYONE

POETRY NOW 2003 - Any subject,
any style, any time.

WOMENSWORDS 2003 - Strictly women,
have your say the female way!

STRONGWORDS 2003 - Warning!
Opinionated and have strong views.
(Not for the faint-hearted)

All poems no longer than 30 lines.
Always welcome! No fee!
Cash Prizes to be won!

Mark your envelope (eg *Poetry Now) 2003*
Send to:
Forward Press Ltd
Remus House, Coltsfoot Drive,
Peterborough, PE2 9JX

**OVER £10,000 POETRY PRIZES
TO BE WON!**

Judging will take place in October 2003